OUT OF THE LAB
EXTREME JOBS IN SCIENCE

MARINE BIOLOGISTS

by Ruth Owen

PowerKiDS
press

New York

Published in 2014 by The Rosen Publishing Group, Inc.
29 East 21st Street, New York, NY 10010

First Edition

Produced for Rosen by Ruby Tuesday Books Ltd
Editor for Ruby Tuesday Books Ltd: Mark J. Sachner
US Editor: Joshua Shadowens
Designer: Emma Randall

Photo Credits:
Cover, 4–5, 4 (bottom left), 7, 8–9, 11, 12–13, 18–19, 21 (top), 23 (bottom),
24–25, 29 © Shutterstock; 1, 18 (left), 21 (bottom), 22–23 © Fiona Ayerst
Underwater Photography; 5 (top) © FLPA; 14–15 © Justin Guariglia/National
Geographic Stock; 17 © Superstock; 26–27 © National Oceanic and Atmospheric
Administration.

Library of Congress Cataloging-in-Publication Data

Owen, Ruth, 1967–
  Marine biologists / By Ruth Owen. — First edition.
     p. cm. — (Out of the lab: extreme jobs in science)
  Includes index.
  ISBN 978-1-4777-1291-7 (library binding) — ISBN 978-1-4777-1381-5 (pbk.) —
  ISBN 978-1-4777-1386-0 (6-pack)
  1. Marine biologists—Juvenile literature. 2. Marine biology—Vocational guidance—
  Juvenile literature. I. Title.
  QH91.45.O94 2014
  578.77'023—dc23
                          2013010581

Manufactured in the United States of America

CPSIA Compliance Information: Batch #S13PK8: For Further Information contact Rosen Publishing, New York, New York at 1-800-237-9932

Contents

A MIDNIGHT TURTLE PATROL

A team of scientists and **volunteers**, led by a young **marine biologist**, José Urteaga, is patrolling a beach in Nicaragua at night. Suddenly, a huge leatherback turtle crawls from the sea.

The turtle is about 6.5 feet (2 m) long and weighs about 1,000 pounds (450 kg), or the same weight as five adult men! In front of the watching scientists, the turtle digs a large nest hole in the sand with her flippers. As the turtle starts laying her eggs in the nest, the team members slip a plastic bag in the hole and catch them. Soon the scientists have darted back into the night. Now, they will take the eggs to a **hatchery** where the eggs will be safe from **poachers** that want to collect them to sell.

Leatherback turtle

Egg

Nest hole

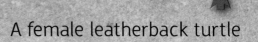

A female leatherback turtle

At a sea turtle hatchery, turtle eggs are buried in nests in the sand dug by scientists or volunteers. The hatchery is then protected by fences and sometimes large nets to stop people or animals from disturbing or stealing the eggs.

Each of the green nets is protecting a clutch of buried turtle eggs at this sea turtle hatchery.

ON THE BRINK OF EXTINCTION?

Before people like José Urteaga began their patrols, poachers raided nearly every turtle egg on the beaches of Nicaragua's Pacific coast. The poachers hunted adult turtles, too.

Sea turtle poachers are people who earn money selling the eggs and turtle meat as food. Turtle shells are also sold for jewelry making. José Urteaga's team protects the turtle eggs at the hatcheries. Then, when the baby turtles hatch from their eggs and emerge from under the sand, the team releases them safely into the ocean.

José doesn't only help the leatherback turtles. He also works with turtle poachers to help them find other ways to earn money, such as beekeeping to produce honey for selling. He has even given ex-poachers jobs on his team.

SCIENCE IN ACTION

Without scientists like José Urteaga protecting leatherback turtle eggs from poachers, these animals, which have been on Earth for more than 100 million years, might be facing **extinction**.

This tiny leatherback turtle hatchling is about to be released into the ocean by a scientist.

WHAT IS A MARINE BIOLOGIST?

Marine biology is the scientific study of plants, animals, and other living things that are found in **marine**, or ocean, environments. A scientist who works in marine biology is called a marine biologist.

Marine biologists study the behavior, lives, diseases, and habitats of marine animals and other **organisms**, such as **fungi** and even **bacteria**. There are plenty of fascinating **species**, or life forms, to study, too!

The World Register of Marine Species is a detailed list of all the known species in the world's oceans. At the beginning of 2013, the register contained details of over 200,000 different marine species. There are many more to be discovered, though, and marine biologists are an essential part of this work.

SCIENCE IN ACTION

New species are added to the World Register of Marine Species all the time. Scientists estimate there may be one million different species living in the world's oceans!

A marine biologist
watching an octopus

An octopus

9

OUT OF THE LAB

Because there are so many different marine species and habitats, most marine biologists have one special area of interest.

For some, their work involves studying tiny living things that can only be seen with a microscope. Others may track or rescue large animals, such as **endangered** sea turtles, or huge whales that become trapped in fishing nets. Many marine biologists, like José Urteaga, choose work that goes a step further. They use their scientific training to improve our planet and the lives of both the animals and humans living here.

A lot of marine biology work takes place in **laboratories**. However, marine biologists may also spend several months a year out of the lab working in or near the ocean.

SCIENCE IN ACTION

Most scientists who work as marine biologists are strong swimmers. They may also need to know how to scuba dive.

Getting up close with a 39-ton
(35-t) humpback whale is all
in a day's work for some
marine biologists!

A SEAL-TAGGING MISSION

Marine biologist Michelle Cronin studies gray seals. One day in 2012, Michelle found herself out of the lab in a boat on the wild Atlantic Ocean.

With her team, Michelle was watching 1,000 adult gray seals. The seals were resting on a beach on a **remote** island off the southwest coast of Ireland. The scientists' mission that day was to capture eight male seals and attach **tagging devices** to them.

It would be impossible to follow a seal day and night in a boat or even wearing scuba-diving gear. Using satellites, however, scientists are able to collect data from a seal's tagging device and track the animal's movements.

Gray seals resting on a beach

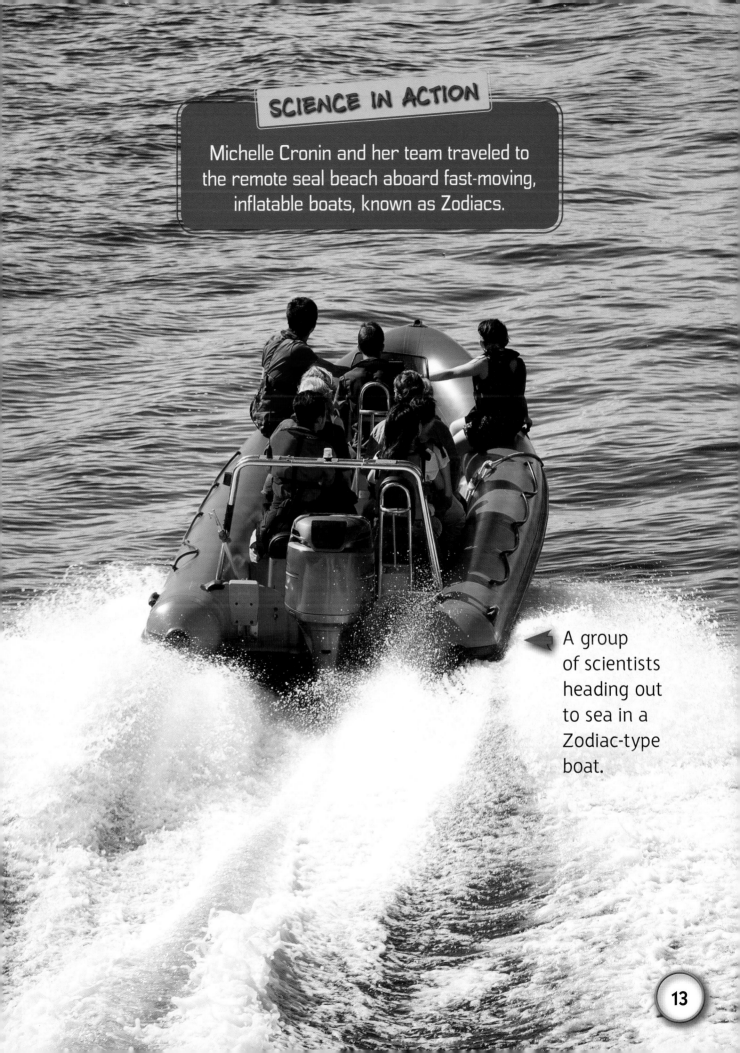

Michelle Cronin and her team traveled to the remote seal beach aboard fast-moving, inflatable boats, known as Zodiacs.

A group of scientists heading out to sea in a Zodiac-type boat.

RUSH AND GRAB

Michelle and her team got close to the shore in their boats. Then they rushed onto the beach.

The scientists used a "rush and grab" approach to capture the animals. In water, seals are graceful and fast-moving. On land, however, they move much more slowly. Michelle's team needed to take the seals by surprise and catch them in nets before the animals escaped into the sea.

Once the eight seals were captured, Michelle injected them with a drug to send them to sleep. Then, she glued a tagging device to the fur of each seal. Once the seals were tagged and awake again, they were released into the ocean.

This gray seal has been captured using a net and is ready to be tagged.

UNCOVERING THE FACTS

Michelle Cronin and her team wanted to find out how gray seals affect the fishing industry. Fish are a seal's natural food, but many people also rely on catching fish to make a living.

If fish numbers in an area start to go down, fishermen may blame seals. Seals also visit fish farms and steal fish from the large netted enclosures where the fish are reared. When seals and people are in competition, people in the fishing industry may ask their government to cull, or kill, the seals. **Conservationists** may argue, however, that fish numbers are low because of overfishing or ocean **pollution**.

It's important that both sides of the argument know all the facts before any decisions are made about how to solve the problem. Tracking seals using tags allows scientists like Michelle Cronin to find out where the animals are finding their food.

The tagging device doesn't hurt the animal or affect its everyday life.

A scientist glues a tagging device to a seal's fur.

SHARK SCIENTIST

Dorsal fin

The marine animals most feared by humans are sharks. New Zealand–born shark scientist Ryan Johnson wants the world to know that sharks have far more to fear from us than we do from them, however.

Sharks are captured and their fins cut off to make sharkfin soup. They are also caught and killed just for sport by anglers.

Ryan studies sharks so he can educate people about these amazing creatures and the important role they play as top **predators** in the world's oceans.

Marine biologist
Ryan Johnson

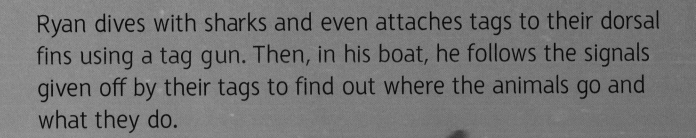

Ryan dives with sharks and even attaches tags to their dorsal fins using a tag gun. Then, in his boat, he follows the signals given off by their tags to find out where the animals go and what they do.

◁ Part of Ryan's job is to dive with great white sharks—the largest predatory fish on Earth!

INTO THE SHARK PIT

Imagine diving in a maze of undersea caves and tunnels knowing that at any moment you could come face to face with a shark. It's all in a day's work for Ryan Johnson.

With his dive guide, Hugh, Ryan searches for "shark pits" in the Indian Ocean. These giant, cavern-like underwater places are where sharks gather. Above each pit, the water bubbles and swirls like a jacuzzi. Inside a shark pit, Ryan can study the sharks' habits and attach tags to them. He even follows the sharks, swimming behind them through underwater tunnels as they move from pit to pit.

There was a mystery, however, that Ryan wanted to solve. Why do sharks gather in shark pits?

SCIENCE IN ACTION

One time Ryan was surprised by a great white shark while diving alone. Ryan had no way to defend himself, but stayed calm and ducked under the animal each time it approached him. Finally, after circling him for 20 minutes, the shark swam away!

A group of divers follows sharks through underwater tunnels and caves.

Ryan Johnson sets off on a dive.

PROTECTING THE SHARK'S WORLD

Ryan and Hugh had a theory that the sharks gathered in the shark pits because of the whirlpools of water in these areas.

The bubbles in the swirling water above the pits could be adding extra oxygen to the seawater. Spending time in water that is foaming with air bubbles would make it easier for the sharks to breathe.

Ryan took samples of water from a shark pit. Back on land, he analyzed the water and discovered it had more oxygen than seawater taken from another part of the ocean. Ryan's research shows that shark pits are an important part of a shark's habitat, so these underwater places must be protected!

Sharks breathe by taking oxygen out of water using body parts called gills. To keep water flowing through their gills, sharks must keep moving. When a shark is in a shark pit, the air bubbles in the water allow the animal to rest more often, but still get enough oxygen.

Ryan Johnson filming sharks

Gills

A great white shark

EXTREME SCUBA DIVING

Marine biologist Rhian Waller studies deep-sea corals.

Usually, Rhian studies these ocean life forms by watching videos made by robotic submarines at great depths. One day, however, deep-sea corals were discovered growing at a depth that was safe for a human to dive to. This meant that Rhian would have the chance to see them up-close. The only problem was they were growing in the icy waters of Alaskan **fjords**!

Rhian's extreme, out-of-the-lab, scuba diving mission took place in water that was nearly freezing. Within five minutes, her face and hands were numb with cold. Also, the water was so murky that at times Rhian couldn't even see her own hands. The extreme conditions were worth it, though, to see and touch deep-sea corals for real!

The icy waters of an Alaskan fjord

A fjord in Alaska

Corals grow in many different colors and shapes in oceans all over the world.

SCIENCE IN ACTION

Many ocean animals and other organisms live on and around reefs formed from coral. Therefore, they are a very important part of the ocean. However, corals are often damaged or destroyed by fishing nets.

TO THE RESCUE

Some marine biologists use their skills and knowledge of ocean animals to carry out rescue work by becoming marine mammal responders.

Sometimes, whales and other large mammals become entangled in fishing gear. When a whale in trouble is spotted, a rescue team speeds to the location in a small inflatable boat. Using hooks on long poles, the responders attach floating buoys to the fishing gear around the whale. The buoys slow the whale down and stop it from diving way below the surface. Then, from their small boat, floating in water above a distressed creature weighing many tons (t), the brave responders use long knives to cut the fishing gear from the whale.

Not every whale can be saved. However, even an unsuccessful rescue attempt can give the responders information that might help a whale next time.

SCIENCE IN ACTION

Like all mammals, a whale needs to breathe air. If it is entangled in fishing gear, it may be pulled underwater and drown. Alternatively, the gear might injure the animal or make it unable to swim well enough to catch its food.

A rescue team reaches a whale entangled in fishing gear.

Whale   Floating buoys

Responders get up-close to a giant creature to cut the fishing gear from its body.

LIFE AS A MARINE BIOLOGIST

As a marine biologist, you might study one of the many known ocean organisms. However, with a million possible species living in the ocean, your work might one day include discovering a completely new life form!

A day's work may involve investigating the effects of pollution or industry on ocean animals and plants. You might study a disease that's destroying marine life forms. You could swim alongside dolphins or gather samples of tiny organisms to view through a microscope. There will be reports to write and educational presentations to give to school children, conservationists, business people, politicians, or other scientists.

When working out of the lab, your working day might also involve being hot, cold, and usually very, very wet!

SCIENCE IN ACTION

Some marine biologists work as curators in aquariums. They feed the animals, care for them when they are sick, and clean the animals' tanks. Aquarium curators also design and sometimes build the display tanks where the fish and other animals live.

This aquarium curator is working underwater building a coral reef inside a display tank.

This marine biologist is checking sea grass for signs of pollution damage.

GLOSSARY

bacteria (bak-TIHR-ee-uh)
Tiny living things that can only be seen with a microscope. Some bacteria can cause disease.

conservationists
(kon-sur-VAY-shun-ists)
People who do work to protect the natural world from damage by humans.

corals (KOR-ulz)
Tiny ocean animals that are joined together. When corals die, their rocklike skeletons remain to form a hard mass of matter known as a coral reef.

endangered (in-DAYN-jerd)
In danger of no longer existing.

extinction (ek-STINGK-shun)
The state of no longer existing.

fjords (fee-YORDZ)
Long, narrow waterways between high cliffs.

fungi (FUHN-jye)
Living things that are neither plants nor animals. Mushrooms and mold are types of fungi.

hatchery (HACH-uh-ree)
A place or building where eggs are kept safe and warm so they hatch either in incubators or, in the case of turtle eggs, by being buried in sand.

laboratories
(LA-buh-ruh-tawr-eez)
Rooms, buildings, and sometimes vehicles, where there is equipment that can be used to carry out experiments and other scientific studies.

marine (muh-REEN)
Having to do with the sea.

marine biologist
(muh-REEN by-AHL-uh-jist)
A scientist who studies living things, such as animals and plants, that live in oceans.

organisms (OR-guh-nih-zumz)
Living things.

poachers (POH-cherz)
People who break the law by killing an animal or taking it from its natural habitat.

pollution (puh-LOO-shun)
Oil, garbage, chemicals, or gases that have escaped into water, air, or onto land and are causing damage.

predators (PREH-duh-terz)
Animals that hunt and kill other animals for food.

remote (ri-MOHT)
Far from towns and cities and difficult to reach.

species (SPEE-sheez)
One type of living thing. The members of a species look alike and can reproduce together.

tagging devices (TAGG-ing dih-VYS-ez)
Small pieces of equipment attached to animals so that they can be tracked using satellites or radio waves.

volunteers (vah-lun-TEERZ)
People who do a job without pay to help others.

WEBSITES

Due to the changing nature of Internet links, PowerKids Press has developed an online list of websites related to the subject of this book. This site is updated regularly. Please use this link to access the list:

www.powerkidslinks.com/olejs/mari/

READ MORE

Peterson, Judy Monroe. *Underwater Explorers: Marine Biologists.* Extreme Scientists. New York: PowerKids Press, 2008.

Thomas, William David. *Marine Biologist.* Cool Careers: Cutting Edge Careers. New York: Gareth Stevens Hi-Lo Must Read!, 2009.

Thompson, Lisa. *Sea Life Scientist: Have You Got What it Takes to Be a Marine Biologist?* On the Job. Minneapolis, MN: Compass Point Books, 2008.

INDEX